ONE MONTH TO LIVE
A Father's Last Words

ONE MONTH TO LIVE
A Father's Last Words

Fran Rogers

"Precious in the sight of the Lord
is the death of his saints."
Psalm 116:15

ONE MONTH TO LIVE

A Father's Last Words

1st Edition

© 2018 Fran Rogers
Father and Family Books
ISBN-13:978-1732681408
ISBN-10:1732681406

godsgracegodsglory.com

Unless otherwise indicated Scripture quotations
are from the Holy Bible, King James Version

Cover by Clara Marsh
Image: pixabay

IN MEMORY

James V. Canady, 1909-1994

He loved his family and worked hard to provide for our needs. He worshipped God. He lived a godly life. He disciplined his children, based on his knowledge of God, of the world and its temptations, and taught us to "fear God" ~ "the beginning of wisdom." Proverbs 1:7

And we loved him.

My earthly father is now "resting in the Lord,"
~ as well are my mother and my brother.
Our heavenly Father continues to care for me
and my family.

And we love Him.

Contents

Introduction
1 Wearing Down 1
2 "He Insisted" 5
3 "I Want Mercy" 7
4 The Diagnosis 13
5 Infusion Complete 17
6 The Past 19
7 "I Want Someone to Hold Me" 21
8 "Whiter Than Snow" 25
9 "I'll See You in the Morning" 29
10 "You Can Let Go" 33
11 "Just a Skeleton" 35
12 Restoration 39
13 A Different Person 43
14 The Back Seat 47
15 The Beginning 51
16 A Year Later 53
The Letter 55
The Last Chapter 61
"We Shall Behold Him" 62
From the Author 63
Acknowledgements 66
Remembering the Former Years with My Dad......67

Introduction

The idea for recording events between August 8 and September 5, 1994, was to share these with Daddy's sisters, especially Nelle, who lived in Nevada. She was unable to see him before he died or to come to his funeral.

As we recalled each day, we realized there were many of God's blessings to be shared. We gave this little book to as many of the family and friends as possible. (Now, twenty-four years later we share this story, hoping that others who are dying, or ministering to a loved one may benefit from our experience.)

We believe that we have the Lord's blessing in this. After Daddy died, it was as if he were, by his own spirit ~ and with God's Spirit prompting ~ saying, "Tell my story."

The purpose of this writing is not to bring glory to Daddy, or to us, but to the Lord, our God, Jesus Christ, and the working of His Holy Spirit.

July, 2018

~ 1 ~

Wearing Down

On Sunday evening, August 7th, 1994 around 10:00, my brother, Buford, called to ask if I could come to Thomaston the next day. Jerry's and my hometown is a two-hour-drive from us

He and Mother had tried during the day, to get Daddy to go to the hospital. His chest pain had gotten worse, spreading into the upper part of his body. He did not want to be taken to the hospital, even though a week earlier he had diagnosed himself as having pneumonia. I learned later that the last time he had been to his doctor he had overheard two men relating experiences of stroke victims dying after contracting pneumonia.

Besides the pain, fear was a very real part of Daddy's life, especially with his heart problems and open-heart surgery in 1980 and his first stroke in 1983. He continually blamed his encounter with cardiovascular surgery; what he called "unnecessary surgery," as the reason for his strokes.

Buford and Mother knew that Daddy needed to see a doctor, but his doctor was out of town the previous week. He had seen another doctor on Wednesday who diagnosed his problem as "a pulled muscle."

The call for me to come was two-fold, I think. One reason: Buford was coming to Atlanta for supplies for his customers on Monday, and he knew that if Daddy was seriously ill, I would want to be there to take him to the doctor. During this conversation, once again, we talked about Daddy's deterioration and the problems for Mother in taking care of him.

For over a year Mother had been Daddy's only caregiver. Even though they had had a young robust woman helping take care of him, who was able to lift Daddy by herself, Mother was now having to help a new sitter coming only in the mornings, who was not able to lift him but needed Mother's help. Buford and his son, Joe, who both lived nearby, came in the evenings to help get Daddy in bed.

This story is not only about God proving Himself in Daddy's life, but also in Mother's; and she gave her permission to relate what I witnessed during the past few years.

There was a time during my visits with Mother and Daddy that Mother's patience and energy were getting faint. Crying was not one of Mother's habits and I knew that things were getting to her. When I would leave to come home, she would hold onto me when I hugged her. She did not cry long after we talked about the "grace" of our Lord. She knew and acknowledged that without His strength she would not have made it that far, nor could she endure much longer. She felt the demands that Daddy made on her. Not only was his outer nature wearing away --- Mother was wearing down, emotionally, too. It was a tough time for all of us; I always left with a heavy heart.

But, after months of prayer, the study of God's working "in the middle of" and being "greater than" our circumstances, I was sharing with Mother what I had learned. She began to draw on God's promises to "always be with us" to be our "help and shield."

She began to "see" Daddy differently, to act more compassionately toward him, and to love him unconditionally. She developed a new sense of humor that she had lost many years before.

The physical hardship did not change. She still had to help lift Daddy and do whatever he wanted. She still had to change his clothes and bed linens often during the night and loads of extra laundry had to be done. But emotionally and spiritually, Mother had something more that carried her through that ordeal and Daddy's death; that continued to carry her through her loneliness. Jesus, her Lord, has proved Himself to be "a very present help in times of trouble," a comforter and a counselor.

~ 2 ~

"He Insisted"

Daddy's doctor was back in his office when I got to Thomaston Monday morning, but was unable to make a diagnosis from his examination. He did not think anything was seriously wrong but suggested chest x-rays which would have to be done at the hospital. He said they would sometimes surprise us.

And he was right. He did not know the results of the x-rays until Tuesday morning. When he called, he told us to bring Daddy to the hospital.

He said he thought Daddy had pneumonia.

Monday night was the last night he slept in his own bed. If he had any idea at the time how close he was to dying, he must not have wanted to die there. When I look back on that morning, I remember how insistent he was every morning that he be helped out of bed. Tuesday morning was no different. And it was the last time and the only time in a long time that I got upset with him. Now I realize that he didn't know what he was doing. He was just following his instinct for survival---fighting to the end.

I was just getting up across the hall. Elizabeth had come and was in the bedroom with Daddy. She was talking to him as if she was trying to get him up. I thought, "Surely he's not trying to get up this morning." In only a few minutes he was sprawled in the floor.

She said, "He insisted that he get up."

I knew then that it was time somebody besides Daddy started making the decisions. How little I knew then that the final decision had been made.

When two men who were nearby at Buford's shop lifted him into his wheelchair, we rolled him to my station wagon and Mother and I took him to the hospital.

~ 3 ~

"I Want Mercy"

Saturdays seemed to be the days that Daddy and I had time alone. God answered my prayers "that Daddy and I could talk about Him and eternity if he needed to."

It never meant that we would talk about "dying." It never happened through my planning nor did it seem that either of us was in control of the conversation.

First of all, there were only a few words on Daddy's part, and when I think back, there is little that I remember saying, although I know that all were encouraging words. The Holy Spirit provided whatever was needed for each time---as Isaiah said, "the tongue to sustain with a word him who is weary" (Isaiah 50:4).

The Saturday that Daddy was in the hospital---the 5th day---he was still not eating. The doctor came late in the afternoon and told Daddy that they could start a feeding tube if he agreed. Mother had gone home to rest.

I told the doctor I didn't know if Daddy understood what he was suggesting. His response was, "Talk to your mother and let me know what you and the family want to do."

After he left, I moved a chair next to the bed, sat down, took Daddy's hand, and said, "Daddy, did you understand what the doctor was saying? Since you are not eating, they want to put a feeding tube into your stomach. Do you know what that means?"

He nodded his head.

"Is this what you want to do?" I asked.

With no hesitation, he shook his head.

"Do you know what will happen if you don't do this?" I said. "It means that you can't get better. You won't get well."

He nodded again to affirm that he understood.

It was an opportune time to say---and without even thinking---as I gently placed my hand on the center of his chest. "There's something there they might not be able to fix."

Although he gave no response, he must already have known. Because he had lost his ability to speak coherently, it seemed that he had given up trying to make us understand what he wanted to say. In the time that we shared that afternoon, he said little. But what he said had deep meaning, for him and for me.

As with all that he said to me in the days left, he spoke clearly. A few minutes later that same afternoon, he said, "I'm afraid."

When I asked what he was afraid of, he said, "The light."

I learned later as I shared this experience with a friend who is a volunteer with Hospice, that it is not unusual for people who are dying to express this fear.

"The light" to me is the wonder-working power of God through Jesus Christ, at work in the world through the hearts of men; but "the light" to a dying person refers to a near-death feeling in which a person sees an unidentified light at the end of a dark tunnel.

I did not think it unusual for Daddy to express this fear, but I responded with thoughts about Jesus, God, and heaven; and I remember saying something about singing in heaven. He had always loved music. Although I never heard him sing, he had always encouraged our family to sing. Growing up, I remember seeing tears in his eyes when he would hear songs about heaven.

I told him that I believed we would all be singing in heaven; that in the "heavenly choir" every person would sing. "No one will sing better than anyone else, but all of us will sing in harmony with Jesus. You and I can sing together."

He cried.

A few minutes later he turned toward me, and simply said, "I want mercy."

I don't remember my response, but his request gave us, the family, the petition that we would place before God, on Daddy's behalf. We know that his request was granted, and God indeed proved that He is a merciful God.

At 5:30, Daddy was looking at the large clock on the wall facing his bed. At 6:00 he looked again.

I asked him why he was looking at the clock.

He said, "To see how much time is left."

He did not look at the clock again.

How can I forget those words? Never before has time meant to me what it does now. Daddy realized in the last days of his life how important time is. His prompting will be a legacy to me and an ever-present part of my living. I believe as Daddy learned, that God gives everyone the right amount of time for all that He has planned. The person who waits until he is dying to learn how to live is wasting precious God-given life. Resisting the power of God's Spirit to make us what He wants us to be is only a prelude to death.

It is in the last stages that we would give up everything to go back and do it all differently.

Andrew Murray, in *Waiting on God*, writes, "The one object for which God gives life to man is that in him, He might prove and show forth His wisdom, power, and goodness." This little book came to me too late to share with Daddy. He would have benefited from it if he could have read it before having several strokes. (Maybe he did understand when he needed to. He tried reading it but gave no indication that he could share what he had read.)

TIME

Time is for living;
Time is for loving.
In the grace of the Lord
He gives us
His life and His love.

Time is for living;
Time is for loving.
In the grace of the Lord,
He gives us the time
To live and to love.

~ 4 ~

The Diagnosis

The doctor ordered more x-rays, and the usual tests that go with respiratory illness, plus EKG, and blood work.

Once in his room, Daddy was hooked up to IV's—one for intravenous feeding and another for antibiotics. Daddy had eaten breakfast at home and had lunch at the hospital—although he was not eating as well as usual. He was getting strangled more often. But, I knew that there was nothing else I could do, so I came back home on Tuesday afternoon for commitments I had on Wednesday and Thursday. Jerry and I would return on Friday, to stay the weekend.

On Wednesday afternoon, Peggy, my sister-in-law, called to tell me that the doctor had told Mother that he didn't think Daddy was going to make it. He thought there was a possibility of cancer. At the time we thought that the cancer was in his lungs. Nothing else was said about cancer until eight days later. During the days following his admittance to the hospital, he was put on the strongest antibiotic available.

Even though pneumonia spread into the other lung, his fever finally subsided, and the doctor said that they would try him without the IV and if the fever stayed down another day, he could release him from the hospital.

Since nothing else had been mentioned about cancer, we were hoping that his first diagnosis had been a mistake.

The day before he scheduled Daddy to be released, Dr. Potitong dropped the "bomb"—final diagnosis: cancer of the esophagus (the reason he had gradually given up trying to eat and was choking, even when he took liquids through a syringe).

"He can go at any time, and I would not count on more than a month."

Within 24 hours we had to decide whether to place Daddy in a nursing home or to bring him home. The Social Services Director was heaven-sent—she contacted and secured a vacancy in a local nursing home (at first, we thought *that* was heaven-sent because it is rare to find an opening). She also contacted the hospice agency that services the Thomaston area.

Thursday night was one of the toughest before we checked Daddy out of the hospital on Friday. With details in mind, Mother and I went home to rest. When we got up and prepared to return to the hospital, the decision had been made. We had both prayed and our thoughts had each taken a different path but the outcome was the same decision.

Mother could not rest because she kept thinking that in the nursing home Daddy would have to be connected to a feeding tube and she knew hr had already decided he did not want that.

My thoughts were more positive as I envisioned setting up the hospital bed in the living room so that people could visit more easily. There was more light than in his bedroom. Since he could no longer get out of bed, he would be closer to us.

The next morning, we met with the Hospice representative, who explained how they minister to terminal patients who choose to die at home. We would have to pay for the cost of sitters and they had to be experienced with patients such as Daddy, who were not able to do anything for themselves.

This cost was the major concern for Buford, Mother, and Daddy. Daddy understood when I told him. His only concern was the money for the sitters. (Until the second week, Mother had not really accepted the doctor's diagnosis. She thought there was a possibility that Daddy would live longer than the prognosis stated.)

The decision was made, and we eagerly prepared for Daddy's homecoming, each one committing to do all we could to make Daddy comfortable. It was not easy. After two days, we wondered if we had made the right decision. The sitters did not work out as well as we had hoped, but finally taking a day at a time, all things came together as other sitters and Hospice worked with Daddy and us.

~ 5 ~

Infusion Complete

We continued to intercede for Daddy—for God's mercy (in any way God was willing to answer that prayer) — and we waited, hoping for some indication that what Daddy needed in his heart and spirit from God was received.

In the meantime, we praised God for all that was being done for Daddy; for the doctors, nurses and the aides, for the family traveling out of town to visit, and for friends who were very supportive during that time.

It was during Daddy's stay in the hospital that they began using a new, computerized instrument for intravenous feeding and medication. Although I had seen this system used in larger hospitals, it was interesting to watch as the head nurse instructed the other nurses on its use. We learned how the system worked as we watched the process, and the nurses, as it took them a while to catch on.

The fluid was programmed to drip from the bags—which were extended above the tubes going into Daddy's body—and when the bags were emptied, the computer would beep and light up with the words, "INFUSION COMPLETE".

The assurance that I had waited for came a day or so later, during the early evening, (Buford and Peggy would sit with Daddy during that time.)

A few weeks earlier I had written an article entitled *The Infusion of Truth*—the thought of how truth from God, through Christ and the Holy Spirit, becomes a part of our being, "eternal life," God's own life, giving new life to our spirit and soul. The hope that what only God could do—in revealing His mercy, His reconciliation, the confidence of God's love for Daddy, the truth of his own salvation and eternity with The Father was revealed to me in an instant. As I lay resting, with my eyes closed, I could see the words INFUSION COMPLETE. Clearly, our Heavenly Father had in His own way, shown that He had indeed given what only He could give—Heavenly manna from above, living water, and healing of the heart and spirit.

Blessings were falling and received every day, in the way God had programmed, and experienced in Daddy, and to me, as spiritual life.

~ 6 ~

The Past

Before Daddy's illness, we knew little about his childhood. He did not talk about it, nor did we know what to ask. During his stay in the hospital, and the news reaching my Aunt Nelle, she talked a long time about Daddy, and the sadness she remembered. The relationship between Daddy and his father was not a good one. Daddy left home when he was sixteen. Hopefully, peace was made between the two before his dad died. He was twenty and Mother was fifteen when they married.

The winter after Daddy died, Mother and I visited Nelle. The following spring, we visited Daddy's two other sisters, Lola and Maude, and Aunt Lula, Daddy's sister-in-law, in Birmingham. It was as if we uncovered a tomb—one in which the whole family had been buried—for lack of love and peace between most of these eight children and a father. Even though Mama Canady was a loving and devout woman, there are still repercussions that remain, continuing into the generations that followed.

We have an understanding we did not have when we were growing up—an ability to see the reasons for things in Daddy's life and our family.

In times past, man's psychology taught me to look for someone else to blame for human inadequacy. Inability to love and be at peace with God and our fellow man is not a one-family failure—it is a worldly failure. The solution is one of Divine origin and work. God, knowing we would need this transformation, planned for it in Christ, by the power of His own Holy Spirit.

This supernatural transformation was working in Daddy before the diagnosis of "terminal cancer."

As father-daughter, we talked about it long before then, and he came to a full understanding during the last three weeks of his life.

If he could be here, and writing this himself, he would say that the last week of this life was his greatest, for it was a springboard into heaven and the presence of his Heavenly Father.

~ 7 ~

"I Want Someone to Hold Me"

H e said, "I want someone to hold me."
These words were the first indication that the man
who was dying of cancer was a different man than the
person we had admitted to the hospital eleven days
before. As long as we had known him, neither
Mother, my brother, Buford, my nephew Joe, nor I
had ever heard or seen Daddy express such a feeling
of need. He had been released from the hospital
Friday, the day before. My niece had driven from
Newman with her mother and eight-month-old son,
John. They had brought cold cuts and trimmings for
dinner, which the whole family, except Daddy, had
enjoyed together.

At first, we didn't think he was aware of what
was going on around him, but every day brought new
experiences that taught us otherwise. His expression
of needing "someone to hold him" came after that
evening meal.

Buford left for a few minutes. Mother and my niece, Cathy, were in the den looking at old family pictures. I had just sat down by Daddy's bed in the living room, taking his hand in mine, when he spoke the words so clearly. He must have been disappointed at my response. If I had not been so surprised, I would have immediately sat beside him on the bed and embraced him.

Because of the doctor's prognosis, my first thought was, "He's dying, and he needs Mother," so I went to get her. She was responsive, her surprise and her thoughts much like mine, but because of the awkwardness of the position, could not actually embrace Daddy either. Sitting next to the bed, she touched him and held him as well as she could. Thinking that Daddy was about to leave us, I asked Cathy to call Buford to come.

Jerry, being more objective than I, suggested that Daddy was aware of the family's togetherness and wanted to be included. For the first time in his life, he revealed to his family his own helplessness and need to be loved.

Others who are knowledgeable of the process of dying have said that it is a time when all that we have experienced, from childhood to the present, comes to the surface. We have nothing to lose by expressing our most deep-seated desires. It is a time when those significant needs are the most easily heard and met—by God and those around us. Daddy's words, "I want someone to hold me," came from the depths of his heart, expressing one of those things that comes from the subconscious, when we are the least in control—with no conscious effort.

A spirit of humility had taken over the spirit of the father we all knew. And we loved him more now than ever before.

~ 8 ~

"Whiter Than Snow"

A day or so after Daddy was home he did not respond to us. Although he had a pulse and a steady heartbeat, we could not get him to open his eyes, or to move.

We thought he was comatose, and so we called Hospice. The nurse came that evening. She too tried but got no response. Afterward, she sat with the family as we gathered in the den.

She informed us that the coma was probably self-induced—Daddy thinking of the trouble he thought he was causing us, the money he was paying the sitters, and his desire to escape the circumstances. She said that he heard everything that was being said, fully aware of all that was happening to him and around him. She suggested that we make him as comfortable as possible. She did not have to tell us to spend as much time with him as we could, encouraging him and assuring him of our love for him.

The nurse and the family left. Soon after, Mother was in the bathroom.

As I was walking down the hall, my spirit was suddenly lifted to sing an old hymn that had been going through my mind, for no apparent reason, the last few weeks.

Lord Jesus, I long to be perfectly whole,
I want thee forever to live in my soul,
Break down every idol, Cast out every foe,
Now, wash me, and I shall be
whiter than snow.
Whiter than snow, yes whiter than snow,
Now, wash me, and I shall be
whiter than snow.

I was joyfully and gently singing the chorus of this song as I came into the living room and was doubly joyful as I saw Daddy's eyes open wide as if awakened by something beyond his own control. I called Mother and we celebrated with Daddy. He knew how happy we were. This song stayed in my heart and on my lips afterward and was used at the funeral as the organ processional.

Daddy did not sleep well before, or after that—his eyes always watching us and all that was going on— although still not responsive, as we would have wanted.

When a few weeks after Daddy's death Psalm 51 was one of my daily readings, I was drawn to the text from which the hymn *Whiter Than Snow* came. As I share part of the Psalm here, you will understand the association of the hymn to our prayer of mercy for Daddy.

"Have mercy upon me, O God,
according to thy loving-kindness; according unto
the multitude of thy tender mercies
blot out my transgressions.
Wash me thoroughly from mine iniquity,
and cleanse me from my sin."
51:1-2

"Purge me with hyssop, and I shall be clean;
Wash me, and I shall be whiter than snow.

Make me hear joy and gladness,
That the bones You have broken may rejoice.
Hide Your face from my sins,
And blot out all my iniquities.

Create in me a clean heart, O God,
And renew a steadfast spirit within me.
Do not cast me away from Your presence,
And do not take Your Holy Spirit from me.

Restore to me the joy of Your salvation,
And uphold me by Your generous Spirit."
51: 7-12

"The sacrifices of God are a broken spirit,
A broken and a contrite heart—
These, O God, You will not despise."
51:17

Daddy must have known this Psalm. It was speaking to and through him, to God, during these last days.

~ 9 ~

"I'll See You in the Morning"

A day or so later, Mother was resting.
As I sat holding Daddy's hand, he said, "I'll see you in the morning."

I do not remember how, or if, I responded. Clearly, his spirit was expressing his deepest thoughts.

Soon after, he said, "I need to go to bed."

Not understanding what he meant, I reminded him that he was in a hospital bed that Hospice had set up in the living room. We wanted him there, I explained, so that he would always know what was going on with the family; that he could look out the big window, and still be a part of everything.

When he said again, "I need to go to bed," I asked him why he needed to go to bed.

He answered, "Because I am dying."

All that I said, in response, is not easy for me to remember, for any time he spoke during those last days was rare, but clear, and to the point, and usually, I was surprised. I do remember that particular afternoon was another opportunity for me to encourage Daddy.

Now he was smiling, and I asked, "Daddy, are you happy?"

And he said, "Yes, but sad, too."

And I asked, "Why are you sad?"

He said, "Because of the end."

Seeing the two-fold experience of his dying and our losing him, I reassured him by sharing what God has been teaching me in the last few years.

     "With every end, there is a new beginning. And every beginning with God is more wonderful than any before."

And he cried.

Those were the last words he spoke.

As I thought about that day, I realized that I had cried alone, and with the family, but not with Daddy. I spent time with him and comforted him but had not shown any sadness.

I thought he should know that he would be missed.

One afternoon later, I didn't know if he could understand what I was saying, but took his hand, and told him, "I will miss you."

Then I cried.

On the Saturday afternoon, two days before he died, Daddy was no longer taking anything. There was blood in his urine, an indication, we were told, of the last stage. His eyes would barely open, even though he seemed not to sleep. His only way of responding—and we asked him only to respond affirmatively—was to squeeze our hand. Holding his hand, I asked Daddy if he could hear me.

—no response.

"Do you want anything?" I asked.

—no response.

"Do you know who I am?"

He did not squeeze my hand, but simply patted the top of my hand with his fingers.

Another afternoon Mother was resting. Jerry and Buford were sitting in the carport, the place where on not-too-hot days the family and friends sat to visit.

Willie, the afternoon sitter had not arrived, and I saw what I did not know was my last blessing of time with Daddy alone.

Getting my Bible and choosing verses from 2 Corinthians 3-4, I read to Daddy.

Then gently touching his chest I prayed, knowing the grace of God through the previous days; thanked God that Daddy was in his hands; that Daddy knew him and was at peace.

There was more to the prayer than can be remembered because the prayer was between God and me, and particularly for Daddy and for that moment, between him and God. There was something going on in God's preparation for Daddy that no one else knew.

~ 10 ~

"You Can Let Go"

I came to understand, during Daddy's illness, that we as a family, those closest to the one who is dying, are to do all we can to aid in their transition from this life to the next.

During the last week, a friend told me of a segment of Prime Time that had featured a nurse who told of her experience with patients who were dying. She said that she sometimes had to do what she thought should be the family's responsibility—to tell the patient that it's okay to die. Some patients hold on even though they are suffering. Some think they are responsible for disappointing their family. Some families hold on and won't let the patient go.

Sunday, September 4th, Lee, Brad, and Ansley came.

Daddy's eyes were partially open and he may have known they were there, but we were not sure. Other family members came and went.

During a brief time that Daddy and I had alone, I whispered to him as I held his hand and gently put my hand on his chest.

"Daddy, you don't have to fight anymore. You can let go anytime you want to. Mother and Buford and I are going to be okay."

Later Willie came into the den to tell us that Daddy had seconds of not breathing. She knew the symptoms and suggested we not bother him by turning him anymore. She had lost her husband two years before. As a 17-year, full-time nurse's aide with a local nursing home, she had seen many terminal patients.

Just as the previous day, we each spent time sitting at Daddy's bedside, holding his hand. By evening we knew that we would all be there with him during the night. We were unsure about having Sallie to come for the night shift since we would be there, but we had her come anyway so that she could bathe him the next morning if she needed to.

~ 11 ~

"Just a Skeleton"

Daddy's breathing was erratic Sunday night. We never knew what to expect—if he would just stop breathing—which the doctor said could happen. He coughed occasionally as if something was trying to stop his breathing.

Since Wednesday we kept turning him from side to side instead of leaving him on his back, (which at first was his favorite position) because he had lapses of breathing that afternoon while on his back. Now he was doing this in any position but still hanging on, all night. And when Sallie was bathing him about 6:25 A.M., she had to turn him on his back.

When Mother stood at the end of the bed, she cried softly, "He's just a skeleton."

I knew at this time that the body that had wasted away was filled full with a spirit that we all wish for while we are living and active, the Spirit that Daddy had been searching for all his life.

I held Daddy as Sallie turned him toward the window and she and Mother began to slide under a new pad and clean draw sheet. Daddy didn't seem to be in pain. He just always looked awkward when he was pushed to one side.

I put one hand on his face and patting him, I told him "It's going to be okay. We'll be through in just a minute."

He coughed, and I took his hand in mine.

Seeing his stillness, I put my other hand on his heart.

I felt no movement.

"There's no need for the sheet," I said, as I let him rest on his back. Sallie and I quickly put his pajama top on him.

I came around the bed to Mother as Sallie said, "He's gone."

Together, Mother and I broke and cried.

Sallie put her arms around us and said, "Cry and let it out."

There were plenty of tears that Monday, 6:30 A.M. September 5, 1994, but in the midst of them, I stood next to Mother at Daddy's bedside and thanked God that he had answered our prayers.

He had been merciful to Daddy and to us—more merciful than Daddy had imagined or than we had prayed for. If Daddy was ever in pain, he did not show it. He was never given morphine. And even more merciful than this, Daddy left this world knowing that his heavenly Father was with him. I believe he left with "a new heart and a new spirit" for a new beginning with Jesus, His Lord.

~ 12 ~

Restoration

Because Daddy had lost so much weight and looked emaciated, I suggested that we have a closed casket. Mother and Buford did not agree with me—so nothing else was said about it.

I have not forgotten how startled I was to walk into the funeral home, and see this 85-year-old man that, in a matter of a few hours since morning, looked years younger. A fresh, full face was shining and so healthy looking. Simply from seeing a picture of Daddy when he was younger, the staff had done an amazing restoration.

We couldn't stop talking about how well Pasley had done their work. I believe it was also God's doing, for it will always be a reminder for me of God's own restoration process during this physical life.

Restoration in Christ

The vision of Christ that God has given us is the picture God uses—not of a face, but a heart and a spirit. In Christ, through His redemptive work, we are made new— "new creatures" with "a new heart and a new spirit".

Men may be able to make men look good to other men, but only God, the creator, and Redeemer can take a sick, tired, dead (in trespasses and sin) body and spirit and give Him His own "eternal life" here and how. He makes us look good to Him, and the transformation does not surprise Him.

Daddy's heart and spirit were restored and made new before he died. The last scene of him in the casket is only a reminder of the promise in Philippians 3:20-21.

"For our citizenship is in heaven, from which we also eagerly wait for the Savior, the Lord Jesus Christ, who will transform our lowly body that it may be conformed to His glorious body, according to the working by which He is able even to subdue all things to Himself."

The following verses apply in the same way as those above. These were shared with Daddy at his bedside and at his funeral.

"...we faint not; but though our outward man perish, yet the inward man is renewed day by day. For our light affliction, which is but for a moment, worketh for us a far more exceeding and eternal weight of glory,
While we look not at the things which are seen, but at the things which are not seen; for the things which are seen are temporal; but the things which are not seen are eternal."
2 Corinthians 4:15-17

*"For we know that if our earthly house
of this tabernacle were dissolved,
we have a building of God,
a house not made with hands,
eternal in the heavens.
For in this we groan, earnestly desiring to be
clothed with our house which is from heaven."
2 Corinthians 5:1-2*

~ 13 ~

A Different Person

There are observations we make as we spend time with people. The longer we know a person the easier to detect anything different. And while other people may be friends or acquaintances, no one knows us as our family knows us. We may be fresh, spirited, witty, seemingly confident, kind and considerate to some people for a short period of time, but we are ourselves for the long haul with those with whom we live.

We knew Daddy lived his last few weeks a different person—a person with a unique nature that he had not had before. And as Mother and I have discussed, this we know; that if daddy could come back to earth today, we would not know him as the same person. He would have the same nature as he had when he was dying.

If I did not personally know of the power of God to change the nature of people, my daddy's story would not be written. I would have placed dishonor on my father's reputation.

But because of the miracle of prayer and the power of God's Holy Spirit to make miraculous things happen in people, I believe that we have God's blessing and the blessing of Daddy's new spirit to support his story.

Those who know or thought they knew Daddy would hopefully accept this as his testimony from the grave and be touched by God to see what He can do in any human life that surrenders completely to Him. Daddy would say that he wished he had learned what he knew, sooner. He would have enjoyed life regardless of his circumstances. He would want us all to let God change us while we are young enough to tell our own story.

I never loved my dad more than during those last two days. It's not easy to explain, but it had something to do with his helplessness. He was totally dependent. He could not speak. He could not eat or drink because he could not swallow. Until Sunday, the last day, he had to be turned every two hours. He was lovable because he needed everybody that was there, and I knew he needed me.

I did not pity him. I only felt compassion that overflowed in a way I had never experienced. He drew me to his need because of his absolute dependence; my love for him was overwhelming. It was not a human daughter-father love. It was a divine love from God, a love that God has for us when we admit our helplessness and appeal to him in total dependence.

No wonder Jesus said, "Come to me, all you who labor and are heavy laden and I will give you rest." There is a love extended to those who admit their need, submit, and accept his love and compassion.

Daddy had been independent and had difficulty seeing more than one point of view. He used to be uncomfortable if things were changed from the way he liked them. He used to be easily embarrassed. Had he still been young and in control, he would have gone to another hospital or another doctor hoping for a different diagnosis.

The Mercy of Doctors and Nurses

For three weeks, he was at the mercy of doctors, nurses, aides, family, and friends. He had no need for privacy or embarrassment. He had no view except the one he was given, no strength or time to change anything he did not like. He accepted things as they were. There was no longer anything in his control. And he died happy because he had finally learned how to let go of everything that had no significance.

His concerns for good health and the things of this world were no longer things he could hold on to and in his helplessness and dependence, he reached for the greater things that His heavenly Father had wanted and waited to give—His own Spirit of peace, joy, and love.

If Daddy could speak to us today, he would tell us how grateful he was to his family and friends.

He knew that he had a wonderful devoted wife for 64 years, that his son and nephew were always near to care for him and Mother. He would say to all of us what he could not express before. And he would tell us he loved us.

Hospice did not pick up the hospital bed until Tuesday afternoon. We were saddened to pass by the door seeing the empty bed until the joy of the Lord caused me to go to Mother's side and remind her that God had lifted Daddy out of that sick bed to Himself.

We no longer looked at the empty bed with sadness but with joy.

~ 14 ~

The Back Seat

In tears I had to turn away from the window Friday afternoon, the day the ambulance brought Daddy home. He had never had to be transported anywhere by a medical vehicle before that afternoon, and this one time was enough to make real the fact that all of Daddy's faculties had failed him. It would only be a matter of time.

It was a reminder of the reality that faced Daddy every day since his first stroke in 1983, which left him with limited use of his right leg, foot, arm, and hand. And from that time and with each stroke afterward, his mental ability lessened.

His main concern in life was getting well and he tried everything he knew to find healing. He placed no confidence in physical therapy. It did not produce results fast enough, so he did not pursue this as an alternative, or part of healing.

He depended on Mother for therapy on his legs, but it was more to keep the movement that he had than for improvement.

He always insisted on spending time in his chair in the den during the daytime, even though this placed a tremendous burden on Mother. His fear was that if he could not leave the bed, he would become invalid.

Tears of Appreciation

When people came, he was touched by their visits. He was where he wanted to be, usually comfortable in his lift-chair in the den. In his last few months he had enjoyed people coming even though he did not communicate well with them. Tears were his way of letting them know that he was glad they were there. I think he realized that people came more often, and he may have begun to sense people's caring during that time, but still was not able to express in words what he felt in his heart.

He kept up with the news although he could not discuss it rationally. Not too long before he developed pneumonia, I was there and when I saw that he was watching the proceedings of the O.J. Simpson trial, I asked him why he was watching, and he said, "To prove that I'm right." When I asked what he meant, he said, "That he'll go free." I did not continue the conversation. Where understanding and logic were limited, I felt no need to pursue the subject.

In those years, it was difficult for him to think positively, leaning toward the worst that can happen, especially in his own life.

There was much hope in my heart that Daddy's outlook would change. I wanted Daddy's and Mother's last years together to be happy; for them to experience the grace, love, and joy that come from God—a first-hand experience that had begun to develop in my own life.

Daddy's inadequacies led him to expect what others could do for him. He always wanted to drive or ride in the front seat.

The second time Daddy had to be transported was the morning he died. We did not see the hearse when it came or when they took his body away. But they drove away with the body of a man whose heart and spirit were changed.

When Jerry and I rode in the back seat of the limousine on the way to the funeral, I thought how pleased he would have been to ride in the back with us. No longer would he need to drive or ride in the front.

He would have loved it.

~ 15 ~

The Beginning

At the last point of death, God, through His Holy Spirit, was holding on to Daddy's spirit to "keep" him from the evil one and his control.

He does not force us, but His timing brings us to Himself. When we yield our spirit to Him, He uses all His power in our defense against the powers of this world and death.

In every day there will be the things of this world—the things of the adversary that will try to hold us—our spirit of life—captive to obey.

When temptation comes, God is using all He has, that we have submitted and consecrated to Him, to hold us close to Him.

The temptation of this world comes in disguise, to our spirits. Things look good to us. The "angel of light" appeals to all our human nature, our wants, and our desires. But the only desire he has for us is our destruction.

We may satisfy ourselves with every want and the things we think we need, but these things only serve to hasten our death.

In joint-spirit, through Jesus Christ, our older brother and Lord, who made it possible for us to know and have the Father's Spirit, death has no claim on us. The sin that results in our death has been conquered through the cross of Christ.

God's power to "keep" us and "hold" us is a power greater than death. It is His life in us that He is keeping and holding.

Daddy did not really know his Heavenly Father until all his will was relinquished to His, but in such a short time that he was helpless, he knew in his heart and spirit where to reach. God's Almighty Spirit and strength held him in His arms until the end, and death was defeated. Daddy finally knew he belonged to, was loved <u>and held</u> by His Father. Daddy's spirit—in union with His—was wrenched from his body of death to be His alone, forever.

~ 16 ~

A Year Later

There were mixed emotions when the family members received the following letter. Only Mother responded, and most knew that I had composed and sent the letter. As dear as she was, and was becoming more and more each day, she understood the letter. Some of the family spoke their feelings to her.

Exactly a year after he died—on Monday, Labor Day—Daddy's death came fresh to my mind, and in my heart. We were to leave on Wednesday for a week's vacation in Florida with our children, their families, and Mother.

My thoughts were not on vacation, but on eternal rest, as on Tuesday, I prayed to the same God I had prayed to before, and during, Daddy's bout with cancer.

My prayer that morning led me to ask God the question, "If Daddy could speak to his family today, Lord, what would he say?" God's answer was, "I will give you the words; write it in a letter and send it."

In this was the sense of preserving what God had revealed to Daddy, not only for him but also for generations to come—starting with those that were there when he died.

What had been lost was restored to our whole family in those few days before he died. The Lord, our God, has proven to me who He is, and desires that our family know about the "inheritance" we have—not only in an earthly father, but in and through Him as our Heavenly Father.

Our legacy is one of Divine love, joy, and peace, here—with God, our loved ones, and our fellow man; and eternity in His presence.

The patriarch of our family is gone, but his creator and redeemer, the living and true God, still lives, in Christ, to bring reconciliation, restoration, new life and holiness, "without which we will not see God", or Daddy and the treasures he is sharing in heaven.

"*Our Father, which art in heaven,* don't let Daddy's death and the death of your Son, Jesus, be in vain for our family. Have mercy on us; open our eyes to see what you revealed to Daddy. In Jesus' name, we pray. Amen."

The Letter

Dear Family,

It has been a year today, since God, our Father, and Jesus, our Lord, with the power of the Holy Spirit wrestled for the last time with the enemy for my spirit, and won—triumphantly—to hold me in His arms, as I had in the past several days been "resting" in total submission to Him.

This letter is not to tell you how beautiful heaven is, or to strengthen your hope in the thought of a place called "Hereafter" but to give you a word from the Father that will draw you to Him and His Son, our Lord Jesus.

From everything that is given to you, there is a source. It is the natural instinct to see, enjoy, and dwell on—to become obsessed by the thing that is given. And when there is a need, the tendency is to dwell on the need. The human weakness is being overwhelmed by what is seen and experienced. It is a spell cast by Satan, himself, and blinds each person to God's power and God, Himself. The human spirit is in poverty and being fed each day the same perpetual deception that is causing malnutrition and death, in God's own children.

Some have to come to the lowest point—facing physical death—before God, the source of all, and the giver and filler of all needs, is seen.

I ask you —I BEG YOU— while my death may still be memorable, look around you.

Where is God in your life?

Is He your Heavenly Father?
Has He revealed Jesus, His Son, to you, as the Savior of your life?
Has Jesus become Lord of your life?
Is your relationship with Him the most important thing in your life?

Jesus is the tie that binds to the Father—"the ladder" (John 1:51), "the door" (John. 10:9), "the way" (John 14:6), the cord—a cording to His will in everything that affects the human life and the eternal spirit. The human flesh and mind hold the human spirit captive until it is totally relinquished to the Spirit of God.

I had to give Him everything that I held in my heart as important—being well, being financially secure, having everything I thought I needed. It is not until God, Himself, becomes all you need that you will understand the reason for physical creation—a heart and mind given to each person, to "know" the creator, not just for the things He gives (John17:3).

To know Him, as Jesus, the elder brother knew Him, is His desire for all His children. Whatever you are holding on to, whatever you hold in your heart and spirit as important—LET IT GO—feelings of past experiences, worries over anything. You cannot believe God, The Father, and be anxious about things in your life at the same time. Constant worry is unbelief and that is perpetual sin against God. "Lay aside every weight" all petty differences and take your stand with Christ in "The unshakable kingdom."

"If you will seek the Lord, thy God, you shall find Him, if you will seek Him with all your heart and with all your soul." Deuteronomy 4:29

Don't wait until you are wasting away, but "By his mercies present your bodies a living sacrifice to Him" (Romans. 12:1-2). "Consider yourselves dead to sin and alive to God," and receive life through Christ who had "the power to lay down His life and then take it up again" for your sake (John 10:18). In "newness of life" (Romans. 6:3) "work out the salvation that He works in you" (Philippians 2:12-13).

Look beyond the physical life and its circumstances, the pains and the problems, and see Jesus on the cross. Join Him there; die to "self" (Luke 9:23-24) and all the needs and desires you have in your heart; leave everything behind and let Him take you to the Father and receive "eternal life" (John 12:50) (John 14:16).

Listen to Jesus say, "Come unto me, and I will give you rest" (Matthew 11:28-29).

"Let not your heart be troubled…" "neither be afraid" (John 14:1, 27).

"Follow me: (Luke 9:23) into the kingdom of heaven. "I give you my peace" (John 14:27).

"I came to you, and go back to The Father, so that I may send the Comforter, The Spirit of Holiness and Truth, to give you abundant life, here and now." (John 10:10) that your joy may be full" (15:12).

Let Him sanctify and purify your heart, and make you holy, as He created you to be, in His image (1 Thessalonians 5:23-24).

Let Him in the face of Christ, "Shine the light of the knowledge of His glory into the darkness of your heart" (2 Corinthians 4:3-4).

Become clay in the "Potter's hands"

Ask for His Holy Spirit, His supernatural power (Luke 11:13).
Ask Him to give you a "new heart and a new spirit" (Ezekiel 36:25-26).
Let Him form "eyes and ears" in your "new creation" (2 Corinthians 5:17) that will enable you to see Him and His power to be what He is—a Holy Heavenly Father, gracious and merciful in His will, to His children.

Be filled with His Spirit of Holiness and peace and let Him put your life in order. "The fruit of the spirit"—

the nature that The Holy Father produces in the human spirit that is yielded wholeheartedly to Him "is love, joy, peace, longsuffering, gentleness, goodness, faith, meekness and temperance." Galatians 5:22-23

Lay your own thoughts aside when you read and study and hear His Word and ask for His Holy Spirit to "guide you into all truth" (John 16:13).

"Be silent unto Him and still before Him." "Be still and know that I am God" (Psalm 46:10).
"Be slow to speak and listen to Him."

"Those who endure to the end shall be saved." "His grace in the new heart and new spirit is sufficient for all endurance (2 Corinthians 12:9).

Let your perfect weakness—in humility—be met by His perfect, Almighty power of Holiness and strength, to do in you what you can never do for yourself.

Let Him, in your relationship, be so close that you will see and experience His love and forgiveness in you, for other people. "Perfect love— "the love of Christ" (Romans 5:5)—drives out fear" (1 John 4:18).

Let Him in Christ, and Christ in you, be "one" (John 17:23) in the Spirit of Holiness.

Heaven is not "Hereafter".

Eternity is from beginning to end. It is "knowing"_in your "new heart and a new spirit" (Ezekiel 36:25-26) the source and creator of heaven and heart.

"Worship Him in the beauty of Holiness," ~ "in spirit and truth" ~ every moment of every day.

"Now" and every day is the day of salvation" (2 Corinthians 6:2). You can be delivered every moment of every day, from whatever holds your spirit and controls your thoughts, desires, and impulses, and be lifted into His Holy presence to realize "heaven" in the middle of your life, WHERE, "IN THE PRESENCE OF THE LORD, THERE IS FULLNESS OF JOY. "Thou wilt show me the path of life…at thy right hand are pleasures for evermore" (Psalm 16:11).

We love you—we'll see you in the morning.　　(J. V.)

September 5, 1995

The Last Chapter

Twenty-four years after Daddy's death, God, our Heavenly Father continues to bless.

"For ye have not received the spirit of bondage again to fear, but ye have received the spirit of adoption, whereby we cry, <u>Abba, father.</u>
(Abba, which is ARAMAIC is equal to our word, "Daddy".)

The Spirit itself beareth witness with our spirit, that we are children of God;
And if children, then heirs; heirs of God, and joint-heirs with Christ;"
Romans 8:15-17

"But we all, with open face beholding as in a glass the glory of the Lord, are changed into the same image from glory to glory even as by the Spirit of the Lord." 2 Corinthians 3:18

We Shall Behold Him

**"We shall behold Him
We shall behold Him
Face to face
In <u>all</u> of His glory.**

**We shall behold Him
We shall behold Him
Face to face
Our Savior and King."**

Dottie Rambo

This was one of Daddy's favorites.
Lee sang this at his funeral.

*There is no end
To God's blessings.*

From the Author

Nine years after thinking that my life was coming to an end, God is still working to reveal Himself to me. At the age of seventy-nine, the new heart He gave me twenty-six years ago is continually being filled with His grace. It is through the power of His will that He has enabled me to live joyfully as a caregiver for members of our family: my father with cancer, my grandchildren, my mother with dementia, and my husband, who is an amputee with heart disease and diabetes. There is no better life than that of serving the Master by serving others.

We began writing these wonderful things of His kingdom so as to provide a legacy for our grandchildren. From file boxes to computer documents we have been publishing since 2016 in books that will be archived for future generations.

They are available for anyone who wants to read of how the Lord works in the hearts and lives of His people as He is preparing us to share His eternal glory. Any profits from sales of our books are designated for missions and charity.

"For the Lord is good, His mercy is everlasting, and His truth endures to all generations." Psalm 100:5

Blog: godsgracegodsglory.com
Facebook: Father and Family Books
Contact: f.rogers@bellsouth.net

FREE EBook
FIRST THINGS That Last FOREVER
(Amazon.com)

For other books,
search Fran Rogers Books

Series **Little Books About the Magnitude of GOD (Published*)**

*FIRST THINGS That Last FOREVER
*TWO FULL PLATES ~ Learning to be a Caregiver
*The Garden of GOD'S WORD ~ The Purpose and Delight of BIBLE STUDY
*The LITTLE BOAT and other Short Stories of GOD'S GRACE
*A Broad Review of Andrew Murray's Humility
*GOD is Our Goal ~ GOD'S Plan for His People

Child Keeping ~ God's Blessing to Parents
Notes on Paul's Letter to the Romans
Legacy of the Seven Psalms + One
God's Grace ~ God's Glory

Series **What the Holy BIBLE Says**

*What the Holy BIBLE Says About LIGHT
What the Holy BIBLE Says About GOD'S WORD
What the Holy BIBLE Says About LIFE

Other Books

* Prayers That Bring the House Down
Waiting is Not a Game~ Articles of Faith
The Master Gardener and other Poems of God's Grace

ACKNOWLEDGEMENTS

I must praise my heavenly Father and my Lord, Jesus Christ with my whole heart, for their presence and guidance during my dad's terminal illness. They showed me how to walk through the valley of the shadow of death with my dad without fear. They were there in the power of the Holy Spirit in a way that I have never seen before or since, leaving me with the peace and assurance that we are not to dread death as we rest in the salvation of Christ, who loved us and gave Himself for us. We look forward to spending eternity with both my fathers in joy and hope for that day of celebration.

      Our heavenly Father has blessed our family with two children, six grandchildren, and two great grandchildren, one of which we must acknowledge and for which we especially praise Him. Kourtney, our second oldest, with the old manuscript from twenty-two years ago, typed and documented this whole book so that we could share it with future generations, and for others who may want to read of this special event in our family. We praise Him for how He is working in all of us for His glory and our joy.

Remembering the Former Years with My Dad

Daddy was always strong and steadfast in whatever he was doing, whether in his job or with his family. He was the third child of eight, the third son, with five younger sisters who looked up to him. The first brother died at the age of 50, the only one with a college degree. The second one died in his sixties with cancer. Daddy was loyal to his widowed mother, who lived with us during the summer months.

I don't remember him ever being fully at peace. Having lived through the Depression, he was anxious at times. After hearing about his childhood, I could understand his anxiety.

Yet, he was a good man, always honest, generous, tenderhearted and led a fruitful life; his work always impeccable. Though he only finished eighth grade, he was very intelligent, able to accomplish anything he set his mind to. He and Mother worked in the textile mills in Alabama, where he was a supervisor in the cloth department. At the same time, he was building houses. When I was twelve he applied for the opening as manager of W.W. Mac Store in Hogansville, Georgia. We lived there a year, then he bought a franchise for the Economy Auto Store in Thomaston. After a few years there, he sold the store and spent the remainder of his years building houses (one church) and later, developed the swimming pool business, which he passed down to Buford.

It was in the first years of his retirement that he devoted his life to his church, serving as a deacon, until his health began to fail. Then, he attended whenever he could and supported the church with his titles and offerings. ❧